How to Speak
Dutchified English

How to Speak Dutchified English

Gary Gates
Cartoons by Jeanine Wine

Good Books

Intercourse, PA 17534

Published by Good Books, Intercourse, PA 17534
Designed by Craig Heisey

How To Speak Dutchified English,
An "Inwaluble" Introduction To An
"Enchoyable" Accent Of The "Inklish Lankwitch"

Table of Contents

Dedication

"This doesn't make any sense," an erudite friend told me when he read the title of this book. "Dutchified English isn't derived from the Dutch language, it's derived from the German language."

He's right, on the surface. The word Dutchified comes from the German word for German: Deutsch. Deutschified English becomes Dutchified English.

This book is dedicated to all those people who at first seem to be talking a little ferhoodled, but who on closer inspection make quite a bit of sense.

Preface

Even presidents have funny accents.

When John F. Kennedy spoke Boston Brahmin, and when Jimmy Carter spoke Southern, they weren't laughed at. They were men who were true to their regional heritage. Their speech added to the richness of our American tongue.

However, if I would become president, I would be somewhat afraid.

I am a Pennsylvania Dutchman. I speak a variety of English known as Dutchified English, a mode of expression typical of my native region and German-Dutch descendants throughout the United States and Canada. Although there is considerable variation in the subtleties of pronunciation and syntax, there are three main components to Dutchified English: 1) English words that are pronounced with a German accent, such as "clod" for cloud and "crotch" for garage; 2) Words derived directly from the German that are unique to English, such as *rutch*, meaning to squirm, and *spritz*, meaning to sprinkle with water; 3) A German syntax that allows for usage of English words in creative ways, such as "the food is all" and "outen the light."

All my life my fellow Dutchmen* and I have been put down for speaking this way. In high school, teachers who came from other parts of the country would criticize the way we spoke. The pressure to conform to conventional speech patterns continued in college and after college by people who believed they spoke in a superior manner. Too many people have tried to make us feel like dumb, uneducated bumpkins. Too many people have tried to make us feel ashamed. Constant pressure is exerted on us to speak like most people speak—in a flattened-out, colorless, homogenized English.

Linguistically speaking, we are treated like second-class citizens.

Enough of this abuse!

Dutchmen, arise! Be proud of our distinctive speech! Our Dutchified English is a delightful, powerful, humorous version of English. Dutch power!

And to all of you non-Dutchmen, open these

pages and enjoy a good laugh with us Dutchmen. Our Dutchified accent is an accent on humor. And we love to share good things. We hope that in reading this book you will not only gain an appreciation of the way we talk, but also learn to enjoy your own version of English, whatever it is.

As you read this book you will not only learn how to speak better, but when an American Dutchman becomes president, you will understand him when he addresses the nation in Dutchified English.

May you laugh along with all of us Dutchmen in our Renaissance.

Being traditionalists, the speakers of Dutchified English understand "man" and its derivatives to be a "cheneric" term for "humankind."

Dictionary of Terms

In the Dictionary section of this book are sentences using only one, or a few, Dutchified words, so that the featured word is evident, and the contextual meaning clear.

Inevitably, varieties result. This is as it should be since diversity abounds in Dutchified English. The many regional enclaves of German-Dutch settlers throughout the United States and Canada, often heavily populated by the Amish and Mennonites, have their own varieties of Dutchified English. The localities, cities and towns within each region have their own sub-varieties. In Pennsylvania, people in Lancaster speak a form of Dutchified English different than that found in Lebanon or Reading. However, there is a common thread to all of them.

The more people distance themselves from their German-Dutch heritage, the less pronounced is their Dutchified English. But in distancing themselves from their roots, they create their own unique, individualized version of Dutchified English. An influence always remains!

A

A-1: A home sales company. "Ding Dong! A-1 calling!"

Abawt: Near, approximately. "That's abawt right."

Achey Belly: An upset stomach. "Lettie eats yogurt for an achey belly."

Ach: An expression of surprise. "Ach, that can't be so!"

Ackryculchur: The science of growing domesticated food plants. "The Amish practice a natural ackry-culchur that will never wear the soil out."

Affritch: Common, typical. "He's just your affritch guy."

Aftawertz: Later. "We went fishing. Aftawertz, we had a fish fry."

Ain't: The proper contraction for "am not"; also used for "isn't" when it makes the sentence more powerful. "Ain't I smart? At least it ain't as bad as saying, 'Are not I smart?'"

Also means the end of. "To get to Samuel's barn go straight along this crooked road until the fence ain't and then turn left."

All: Finished; gone. "Is the turkey all?"

Also: "When the little red box comes then the train's all."

Altchebra: A branch of mathematics. "Pop! Guess what? I calculated the walue of Y in altchebra class today!"

Alumium: A metal. "We wrap our leftovers in alumium foil."

Alveese: All the time. "Vee alveese go to church on Sunday."

Amonk: To be with a group. "Are you amonk those who are coming with?"

Analysis: The author's wife's name in the present active tense. "My Mom's cooking the turkey analysis bringing the filling for Thanksgiving dinner."

Ankle: An approach; a vector. "A right ankle has ninety degrees."

Anudder: Not this one. "If your car breaks dawn, you can always get anudder."

Ape: A man's name. "Ape Lincoln saved the Union."

Apple Busser: A delicious brown spread made from cooked apples. "Spread me all over with apple busser a piece of bread."

Arawnd: On all sides of; abawt. "These youngsters sure get arawnd these days."

Are: Sixty minutes. "It'll take me an are to get there."

As: Instead of. "Nellie as soon would marry Paul as keep house for him."

A circle can be dewided by four right ankles.

Awch: A cry of pain. "Awch! That hurtss!"

Awt: The opposite of in; also to go unconscious. "He went awt like a light."

Ax: To pose a question. "I don't know. Why don't you ax him?"

B

Back: A paper sack used for carrying things. "My son likes to go Trick or Treating on Halloween and get his back filled with goodies."

Also a place where there's always more of something. "Eat all you like; there's more back!"

Bacon: The act of making bread and cakes. "Ann is a whiz at bacon cakes."

Bass: To clean or wash a person. "Be sure to give your daughter a bass before you put on her new dress."

Bat: Not good. "He was a bat boy yesterday, so I had to spank him goot."

Batch: A symbolic pin worn as a sign of membership. "When the cop showed me his batch, I answered his questions."

Beardy Men: Men with beards. "Married Amishmen

and the guitarists in ZZ Top are examples of beardy men."

Beance: A kind of food. "Beance sometimes eat out loud."

Bet: What you sleep on. "Paul was tired, so he went to bet early."

Bice: To purchase. "Emma bice her groceries at the farmer's market."

Binko Hall: A place where every now and then people yell, "Binko!"

Bissy: Active. "Are you bissy tonight?"

Black Bumper Gang: What some wags used to call some Mennonites because they painted their chrome fenders black. Now, of course, every car has black bumpers. Just goes to show the influence of a powerful idea.

Bleed: To argue for. "My lawyer is going to bleed my case in court Friday."

Bloss: A woman's shirt. "Her bloss is too bright for my taste."

Bond: Liable to. "With all his energy, he's bond to succeed."

Bop: A man's name. "Do you like Bop Jones?"

Bookie: What you sometimes find up your nose. "Jacob threw a bookie on the floor! I saw him too!"

Bose: Inclusive of two things. "Used to be I couldn't say norse or souse, but now I can say bose."

Cherry britches the cheneration gap.

Bra: The forehead. "A farmer earns his money by the sweat of his bra."

Braince: Head noodles. "Use your braince; don't waste them."

Brawn: A color. "Sally always wears a brawn dress to bake pies in."

Bray: To talk with God. "Most people only bray to God when they're in trouble."

Brink: To convey; to carry. "We're brinking the cheese. What are you going to brink?"

Britches: Structures people use to cross rivers. "Lots of old britches are decaying and aren't safe to use anymore."

Brunts: An alloy of metal. "In history class ve learned about the Brunts Age."

Bruise: A man's name. "Nellie buys all of Bruise Springsteen's alpums."

Brutz: To pout. "After our son was spanked, he brutzed for ares."

Buck: An insect. "I hate it in the summer when all those bucks smash against your car. It's tough to wash them off."

Bull: The opposite of push. "I can bull my own weight arawnd here."

Bulps: Onion-shaped objects. "It's dark in here. You need new light bulps."

Bumper: A flying machine used to drop explosive devices called bumps. "My friend Steve served in the 99th Bumper Diwision in the Air Force."

Bunnit: A woman's hat. "Sadie wears her bunnit every Easter only now."

Bush: A shove. "Can you give me a bush? I need to get my car started."

Bus: To make a whiny noise. "Does the bussing of bees in your ear bother you?"

C

Cap: A commercial vehicle. "Do you take the bus or do you take a cap?"

Caw: A bovine animal. "Sarah still milks her caw by hand."

Cello: A type of food. "I like a good strawberry cello for dessert."

Cheap: A type of vehicle. "To get to our cabin we have to drive a cheap."

Cheneration of Wipers: A group of wicked people who are all about the same age. "Our preacher warned us about the dangers of becoming a cheneration of wipers."

"Get out the buck spray!"

23

Chermins: People from Cherminy. "Most of our forefathers in this area were Chermins."

Cherry: A man's name. "My favorite comedian is Cherry Lewis."

Choke: A funny story. "It's an art to deliver a good choke."

Chop: An occupation. "All he needs to get going in life is a good chop."

Choy: An elated feeling. "My family fills me with choy."

Chuck: A container used to hold liquids. "We like to get together and share a frosty chuck of birch beer on hot summer days."

Chuckler Wayne: A major blood vessel. "Can you feel the chuckler wayne in your neck?"

Chump: To leap. "Don't chump in before you know what you're getting into."

Chunk: Garbage, refuse. "Some people think modern art is just a lot of chunk."

Chust: Only. "Chust a little more pie, please."

Clod: White puffs of water vapor in the air. "I wandered, lonely as a clod."

Close: What we wear. "Katie is washing her close in the sink."

Clup: An exclusive group. "Groucho Marx wouldn't join any clup that would have him as a member."

Collitch: An institution of higher learning. "I can speak so much better since I went to collitch."

Colt: Opposite of hot. "I like the colt because I'm a skier."

Crick: A tributary to a river. "We caught some crayfish in the crick."

Crip: What a baby sleeps in. "We put the baby in the crip every night at eight o'clock."

Crod: A large group of people. "What a crod! Everybody in town must've come!"

Crutch: To hold a bad opinion of; resentment. "Nick holds a crutch against Ben and won't go with him anywhere."

Crotch: A building in which cars are kept. "My husband is working over in Amos' crotch helping him to fix a flat tire."

Cummin Sense: What everybody knows. "Why, it's only cummin sense you don't do it like that!"

Cun: To deceive. "That shyster's trying to cun you out of your money."

Cunked Awt: To give awt; to break dawn. "My car cunked awt on me last night and I had to walk twenty miles home."

Cuntack: A connection; also a small optical lense. "Bill's cuntack popped awt when he was playing basketball last night."

"For such a big crotch he sure has a small wehicle."

Cuppert: A kitchen cabinet. "After you dry the dishes, stack them in the cuppert."

Cussin: A relative. "My cussin is fun to play with."

D

Damitch: Hurt or harm. "The damitch to the barn from fire was extensive."

Also: "He's going to sue for damitches."

Dasselt: To have impressed mightily. "Houdini dasselt the audiences with his daring escapes."

Dairsent: Not allowed to. "I dairsent smoke in school."

Dawn: The opposite of up. "Dawn by the river where the britch meets is where Harry fishes."

Debt: Deceased. "Barbara's been amonk the debt for some time."

Dents: Places where lions live and men brood. "Harold has so much stuff, he has two dents in the hawse."

Dewide: To distribute, apportion. "Be sure you dewide the candy equally between the children or they'll be sure to fuss."

Also a boundary that splits something in two.

"Last summer ve drove over the Continental Dewide."

Dick: To bore into the earth. "When did Scott dick his well?"

Also to investigate. "I'm going to dick into that mystery and find awt."

Dippy Eck: An eck fried sunnyside up. (See **Eck**).

Dissy: Off balance. "When I climb too high I get dissy."

Also: "Dissy Dean was a great baseball player."

Donut: Ain't. "This cake sure eats good, donut?"

Dootle: Draw aimlessly. "You can't just dootle in life if you want to make a work of art."

Doppick: Dumb; not too smart. "Chester is so doppick he can't barely run his car, much less a farm."

Dotch: A make of car. "Fannie loves her new black Dotch, it rides so fine."

Drainitch: What takes the water off. "This drainitch system doesn't work so awful good. Ve need new pipes."

Dretch: Low life. "Ve must help lift people out of the dretches of existence."

Drife: To pilot a car. "Do you want to drife?"

Duck: Past tense of dick. "Is the well duck yet?"

Dunnult: A man's name. "Dunnult Duck is my son's favorite cartoon."

Dupple: Two of. "Twins are dupple people."

Burying the debt.

E

Eck: What a hen lays. "Dip your toast in the dippy eck to see what good is!"

Eck Nock: A Christmas drink made with milk, eck, and rum. "Pop's eck nock tastes wonderful good!"

Etchicated: To be well learnt. "I want my daughter to be better etchicated than I am, that's for sure."

Eefning: After afternoon and before night. "The sunset glowed pretty and gave us a beautiful eefning."

Effry: All of them; each one. "Ve eat a good breakfast effry morning."

Enchineer: A person who drives a train. "As kids, ve'd vave to get the enchineer to blast the vhistle for us."

Erased: A man who drives too fast. "Erased a car in the Grand Prix!"

Erector: To have demolished something. "You know Chakie's new car? Erector!"

Et: To have eaten. "Chunny's et himself full already for the night."

Etch: A border or boundary. "Some people thought Columbus would sail over the etch of the world."

Ewade: Avoid. "Don't try to ewade the issue."

F

Faar: Combustion; flames. "Vhere there's smoke, there's faar."

Face: Belief; religious conwiction. "Praise be! Rebecca has found her face in the Lord again!"

False: What water does. "Ve honeymooned at Niagra False."

Famly: A related group of people. "Without a famly, I'd be nothing."

Fausnacht: A donut. "Sarah dunks a fausnacht in her coffee in the morning."

Fergib: To pardon, excuse. "Ve must fergib those who trespass against us."

Ferginny: An American state. "Chorch Washington was born in Ferginny."

Ferhoodle: To perplex, puzzle. "Calculus class sure ferhoodles me."

Fife: One more than four. "There are fife days in a work week."

File: Poultry. "Turkeys sure are an ugly looking file."

   Also unpleasant, putrid: "Vhat is that file odor?"

Fill: To touch. "Let me fill your silky hair."

Filling: What everybody else calls stuffing. "Do you

prefer sausage or potato filling in the turkey at Thanksgiving?"

Finker: A digit on your hand. "If you buy your sweetheart a ring, make sure it fits her finker."

Fiss: What carbonated drinks do. "Vhen you put ice cream in a Coke, it really fisses, ain't?"

Fix: Cook. "Honey, can you fix me some eggs? I haf to eat and run quick."

Flar: Grawnd wheat used in baking. "Add two cups of flar to the batter and it'll thicken up good."

Flack: What flies on a flackpole. "Don't you get a lump in your throat vhenever you salute the flack?"

Fond: To have discovered. "I'm glad Columbus fond America instead of China. Othervise, I don't know vhere I'd be living."

For So: For the fun of it. "Do you vant to go steady, or chust for so?"

Frawn: A negative facial expression. "Vhy do some people frawn at us, Pop?"

Futch: A type of candy or chocolate sauce. "I like my hot futch sundaes with a cherry on top."

G

Garbitch: Refuse; junk. "I hate taking out the garbitch."

Garklin: Rinsing the back of your throat with mouthwash. "Ve always hear our Dad garklin in the morning."

Get Awt: An expression of surprise. "Get awt! I never said that!"

Gluff: An article of clothing worn on the hand to protect it. "I always vear rupper gluffs to do the dishes."

Gookamoedoe: Look at that. "Gookamoedoe! Zachariah and Amy are giving each other the eye!"

Goot: The opposite of bad. "I love to curl up with a goot book."

Got: The divine being. "I thank Got for all I have."

Go To: Take to something. "If your children go to books, you'd better be quick for some good questions."

Grackers: Unleavened bread. "Graham grackers are great, but not in soup."

Graiffy: Sauce from meat cookings. "Do you like graiffy bread?"

Graadiate: To earn an academic degree or diploma. "Sadie did real good in her studies and she's going

to graadiate from Kutztawn State Collitch next
week."

Grawch: Someone who gripes. "Don't let him get
you dawn, he's chust an old grawch."

Grawnd: Earth, soil. "Lankister Cawnty has some of
the best grawnd in the world for growing things."

Grex: To complain; moan. "Ah, quit your grexing,
you have a vonderful life."

Grum: The guy who marries the bride. "I was only a
grum one time, and that was enough."

Gruntbecky: An expression of hard going. "Gruntbecky! It's difficult to run in this hot sun."

Gunked Up: To smear grease on. "If you get those
ball bearings gunked up your bike'll run
smoother."

H

H: Number of years a person or a thing has. "Vhat's
your H?"
Also: "Mattie, is this cheese properly H'd?"

Hank: Dangle; suspend. "Vhere should I hank my
coat?"

Har: A terrible disgust or fright. "Har movies are
scary."

Hawse: Where Pennsylwania Dutchmen dwell. "Come on over to our hawse."

Also a question: "Hawse the weather today?"

Haw: In what manner or way. "Haw much do you want for this?"

Heart: Not easy. "Emma's got a heart life."

Heef: To forcefully throw. "Heef this ballast over the side to lighten the ship."

Heel: Elevated ground; a knoll. "Daniel ran up that heel without stopping?"

Heffen: Where you go if you're good. "Vill I be seeing you in heffen?"

Height: Conceal. "Vhere can you height an elephant?"

Herititch: Tradition. "Our American herititch is amacing."

Het: The round thing on top of your neck. "If you don't use your het to get ahet, you're bond to fail."

Hex Sign: A rawnd sign with a pretty design meant to scare away the devil and make a barn look pretty. "Josh's barn got a new hex sign yet."

Hock: A large swine. "Levi gets good pork from his hocks."

Hoppy: A recreation activity. "Do you have any hoppies? My hoppy's coin collecting."

Huck: An affectionate squeeze. "Come and give your aunt a big huck!"

35

Hun: A sweetheart. "I'm going to the concert to-night with my hun."

Hunert: Ten tens. "I hope to live to be a hunert."

Hunk: Past tense of hank. "He was hunk for his crimes."

Hunkry: Famished; starved. "I'm so hunkry I could eat a horse."

Hurrieder: Faster. "The hurrieder I go, the behinder I get."

I

Ice: What you see with. "Craig has green ice in his head."

 Also: "My, what pretty ice you have!"

Imitch: A projection, shadow, or replica of. "He's going to have to project a better imitch if he wants this chop."

Immejitly: Right away. "Aaron! You stop kicking her immejitly!"

In: At the place of. "He turns the gate in to get to the store."

Indiwisiple: Not dewisiple. "This nation is one nation, indiwisiple."

Wan Go: See definition of "Inwaluble."

Indiwitchally: By oneself. "They drove indiwitchally."

Infectious: A woman who is indeed doing something. "Is she in school? Vhy sure, infectious working on her doctorate yet."

Injun: A motor. "You'll need a good mechanic to fix your injun."

Inklish: A lankwitch, or a person from Inkland. "His Inklish isn't so good."

Innilect: Brains. "Einstein was a man of high innilect."

Innockilate: Vaccinate. "The kids get innockilated in school."

Intellichintz: Brains. "An IQ test tests your intellichintz."

Inntrest: Money earned on a loan. "My bank pays good inntrest."

Inwade: To attack a place to occupy it. "It was a mistake for Napoleon to inwade Russia."

Inwaluble: Priceless. "A painting by Wan Go is inwaluble."

Inwariable: Not warying. "The speed of light is inwariable in any medium."

Inwent: Create. "Inwent a perpetual-motion machine? I'm too tired."

Inwestigate: Look into; explore. "Man is meant to inwestigate the heavens."

Inwhite: Ask over. "Did you inwhite the Smiths for supper?"

Inwolve: To include; to make a part of. "I don't vant to get inwolved."

Iragoy: An Indian tribe. "The Iragoy were a north voods people."

J

Jap: Punch. "Kevin threw a jap at me when I told him what I thought of him."

Japder: A division of a book. "The hero rescues the maiden in japder nine."

Jams: Night close. "Go put on your jams, it's time to go to bet."

Jewelery: Adornments for the body. "Even men wear jewelery these days."

Jinkle: The sound small bells make. "Jinkle bells! Jinkle bells! Jinkle all da vay!"

Jock: To run slowly. "There's nothing like a good jock to keep you in shape."

Jutch: Criticize. "Jutch not that you be not jutched."

K

Keel: Slay. "If I would have had a gun the other day, I could have keeled a deer."

Also: "Thou shalt not keel."

Ken: To be able to. "Ken you run the mile in six minutes? Kenny ken!"

Kenya: Are you able. "Kenya come?"

Ketch: To grasp. "Did you ketch what that eckhead said?"

Also: "Let's go awtside and ketch ball."

Also: "You'll ketch it if your Mom finds awt."

Kilt: To have keeled. "Carl kilt a bear last hunting season."

Kink: The ruler of a country. "Prince Charles will someday become the next Kink of Inkland."

Kits: Children. "How many kits do you have? I have four kits, and they drife me crazy!"

Knack: An old horse. "Did you buy that knack at the auction?"

Also to pester or harass: "All my vife does is knack when I'm home."

Knowed: To have the acquaintance of. "Did you think you knowed me?"

Kumpis: An instrument that tells direction. "If you

Last year Run kilt a bear.

go alone into the vilderness, take a kumpis with you."

Kumpny: Wisitors. "We're having kumpny over for supper tonight."

L

Lacy: Not active. "Tom is so lacy, he got a goat to mow his lawn."

Lankister Cawnty: The heartland of Pennsylwania Dutch country, commonly misspelled on maps as "Lancaster County." "I wish they all could be Lankister Cawnty girls."

Lankwitch: A system of speech. "I still can't make awt what fer lankwitch he uses yet."

Larch: Not small. "That's a larch tree."
"No, that's an oak."
"I know, it's a larch oak."

Lasty: Durable, long-lasting. "Bluecheens are wery lasty trawsers."

Lawd: High wolume sawnd. "For cryin' awt lawd, you shoulda known better."

Launch: To relax. "Pop likes to launch in his easy chair at night."

Leaf: To go away or to be gone. "Leaf me alone!"

42

A rupdawn is good for a missreple kink.

Learnt: To have grasped a supject. "I sure learnt a lot of Inklish in high school. Did you?"

Lecks: What you walk on. "My lecks are weary from standing on market all day."

Lentz: A piece of glass used to refocus light. "His lentz popped out of his glasses."

Lepnin: A tawn in central Pennsylwania famous for the best bologna in the world. "I'm not hunkry anymore, but I sure could eat some more Lepnin boloney with ketchep on it."

   Also a country in the Mideast. "Those hichackers make Lepnin a dangerous place to wisit."

Libber: A body organ. "There's nothing like eating a good piece of libber for supper."

Liff: Dwell, survive. "Vhere do you liff? In a hawse?"

Little: A small amount of. "I only want a little." "Come over for a little."

Lochencher: A cough drop. "Suck on this lochencher for relief."

Loose: To misplace something. "Did you loose your wallet again?"

Looser: A famous Reformer. "Looser was excommunicated from the Roman Catholic Church for his ideas."

Lotch: A country cabin or a clup. "Pete likes to go to the lotch with the boys whenever he ken."

Mom and Pop like to launch arawnd on Sunday
afternoon.

Also to stay with. "Why not lotch with us tonight?"

Luckitch: Bagitch; a collection of suitcases. "Does effrything you need to travel fit in your luckitch?"

Luff: The greatest feeling in the world. "Fill your heart with luff!"

Also what people fall in. "Mary and Isaac are in luff."

Lunks: What your breathe with. "You need big lunks on you to swim underwater for more than two minutes."

M

Make: An all purpose word for action. "Make the window shut." "Make the dirt away." "The doorbell don't make."

Make Awt: To turn off. "Make awt the light. I want to sleep!"

Also to turn on: "Esther and Bill were making awt and got so excited they missed the bus."

Make Dawn: To rain. "Take your umbrella, it's making dawn awtside."

Mal: 5,280 feet. "I'd walk a million mals, for one of

your smals . . ."

Manitch: To run in an organized manner. "You have to learn how to manitch yourself before you can manitch others."

Manury: Full of natural fertilizer. "That scheme is manury."

Maple: A woman's name. "Maple luffs Cherry."

Maritch: Matrimony. "Maritch can be a lot of hard work."

Mate: Constructed, built. "Rose mate this quilt with her own hands."

Mawntins: Larch hills covered with trees. "Ve haff a cabin in the mawntins for wacation."

Mawse: A small rodent. "A mawse lives in our bedroom wall."

Mawth: What food goes into and sawnd comes awt of. "Ach, shut your mawth!"

Maychur: A military rank. "Richard's a maychur in the Green Berets."

McDunultz: A fast food chain. "Ve take the famly to McDunultz for Bic Macs."

Meal: A place where grain is crushed. "They mate a restrent awt of the olt meal dawn by the stream."

Meppy: Perhaps. "Meppy I will, and meppy I won't."

Missreple: Unhappy, uncomfortable. "Stop being so missreple."

Mohegans: An Indian tribe. "James Fennimore Cooper wrote "The Last of the Mohegans."

Moof: Relocate. "I hate to moof."

Moofies: Films. "People like to eat popcorn when they go to the moofies."

Morkitch: A loan on a hawse. "Six more payments and my morkitch is all!"

Muck: A large cup. "A muck of coffee gets you going in the morning."

Mutt: Wet grawnd. "Children luff to play in the mutt. That's not too bat, but you have to mind they don't eat mutt pies yet."

N

Nalentz: Ladies' hosiery. "Excuse me, but there's a runner in your nalentz."

Nassaress: The town where Jesus grew up. "Nassaress is in the Holy Land yet."

Natchral: Normal, not artificial. "It's only natchral to speak dis vay."

Naw: An expression of disbelief. "Naw come on!" Also, right away: "I want it done naw."

Needer: Not one or the other. "Needer one of them will budge."

Nerf: A neuron that controls the movements of muscles. "You have to have good nerfs to be a surgeon."

Nix Nootz: A devilish, mischievious person. "Our daughter is a little nix nootz."

No: Any. "I don't got no melons today."

Noah: Used to emphasize the negative. "Did I do it? Noah!"

Nohaw: No way. "This relationship's no good nohaw."

Noiss: Sawnd. "What's that noiss?"

Nootles: What Pennsylwania Dutchmen eat when other people are eating pasta. "Eck nootles make a body full."

Noose: Current events. "I watch the CBS noose effry night. Sometimes that daily noose gets depressing. But I always read *The Lepnin Daily Noose*."

Nootzer: A big marble. "One nootzer is worth five smaller marbles."

Norse: A direction opposite of souse. "Santa Claus lives at the Norse Pole."

Nowember: The eleventh month. "Hunting season starts in Nowember."

Nun: The total lack of; zero. "After Linda ate the last apple, we had nun."

Nutzed Up: Messed up. "The President's got the budget all nutzed up."

Nutzin' Arawnd: Goofing arawnd; fooling arawnd. "If you don't have anything better to do, you often end up chust nutzin' arawnd."

O

Oafer: Above. "Somewhere, oafer the rainbow . . ."

Odder: An aquatic animal. "Odders sure are playful in the water."

Off: Wacation time. "My off is all until next year." Also no trespassing: "Keep the grass off!"

Olt: The opposite of yunk. "Ve grow too soon olt, and too late smart."

Opchect: A thing, a point. "Vhat's the opchect of this lesson?"

Oranch: A fruit from Florida. "Oranch choose is best for breakfast."

Ott: Unusual. "Some people sure speak ott."

Ouches: Hurts, pains. "This cut ouches me so."

Outen: To turn off; extinguish. "Outen the light, I want to go to sleep."

P

Pawder: Talcum. "Vhat's the vite stuff on your neck? Vhy, it's pawder!"

Pal: A heap; a stack. "Put that wood in a pal so it doesn't take up the whole yard yet."
   Also: "Make a pal with those boxes."

Packitch: A parcel. "Take these packitches over to your Aunt Martha's."

Paitch: What this is written on. "Turn the paitch when you're finished for more."

Par: Force, energy. "He is a man of great par."
   Also: "Does your car have par steering?"

Pawt: To frawn; to brood. "He pawts when he doesn't get his own vay."

Peace: Green things that come in a pod. "You must eat your peace before you get dessert."

Peck: A short wooden rod. "Hang your coat on the peck."

Peel: A medicinal tablet. "Swallow your peels and you'll feel better."

Peep peeps: Baby chickens. "Kids love to get peep peeps for Easter."

Pennsylwania: A state of the Union commonly mis-spelled as "Pennsylvania." "Come to Pennsylwania and enchoy yourself."

Pick: A small swine. "Do you make bacon from your butchered picks?"

Pichur: A photograph. "Who's that lady in the pichur?"

Plah: To put furrows in a field. "Ezekiel still uses horses to plah with."

Pleece: The magic word. "May I pleece have some more ice cream, Mom?"

Pletch: To give an oath. "Do they say the Pletch of Allechance in school anymore?"

Prod: To take pleasure in something. "Most people are prod to be Americans."

Powvower: A folk medicine healer. "A powvower cured my mom from scarlet fever when she was a beppy."

Precedent: The man in charge. "A Dutchman would be a good precedent."

Produse: Foodstuffs. "Farmer's market has the freshest produse."

Prum: A high school dance. "Bill's taking Sue to the prum this year."

Prumiss: To pledge; swear. "Do you prumiss to love her til death do you part?"

Punnyack: A make of car. "A chief vas the hood ornament on a Punnyack."

Pup: An English bar. "In London, we drank some beer in a pup."

Purse: A cat's murmur. "She's soothed by the kitten's purse."

Q

Quiss: A quickie exam. "Did you pass that last quiss in class?"

R

Rawnd: Circular. "Columbus thought the world was rawnd before most people."

Receipt: A list of ingredients in a particular food. "May I have the receipt for this delicious shoo-fly pie?"

Reckler: Ordinary. "He's chust a reckler fellow."

Red: To clean or straighten up. "Red up your room before kumpny comes."

Restrent: A place where people eat out. "That restrent has home cooking!"

Rhett: A primary color. "The new firetruck is rhett."

Donnult lets out Grandma's secret receipt.

Rhum: Part of a house. "Go to your rhum and stay there till I say!"

Rice: Comes up. "Where does the sun rice?"

Rick: Equip, prepare. "Ken you rick my yacht for a rawnd-the-world trip?"

Rink: A rawnd metal band worn on a finger. "Cyrus gave Velma a rink for Christmas."

Rips: Bones that cover the lunks. "Don't tickle me in the rips!"

Ritch: A mawntin range. "From up on that ritch you ken see twenty mals."

Rocket: To shake something back and forth. "If you want to stay safe in a canoe, don't rocket."

Romanic: Passionate; in a loving, appreciative mood. "Lord Byron was a romanic poet."

Rot: A wooden staff. "Choe borrowed my fishing rot."

Ruck: Soft material that covers a floor. "Wipe your shoes on that ruck."

Ruint: Spoiled. "Those steaks were ruint when you burnt them."

Rummitch sale: A sale of used stuff. "He's so cheap he buys his close at rummitch sales."

Run: A man's name. "Pop, is Reagan's first name Run?"

Rupdawn: A massage. "A goot rupdawn will take

the ache away."

Rupper: A polymer of isoprene. "Rupper boots will keep your feet dry."

Ruse: A woman's name. "My mom likes to read abawt Ruse in the Bible."

Rutch: To squirm. "Ted! Stop rutching in the pew and listen to the sermon."

Ruts: A famly's heritich. "Our ruts go back to Cherminy."

Also the part of a plant that holds it in the grawnd: "A man is like a plant. If he doesn't put dawn ruts someplace, he'll never grow."

Ruff: The top of a hause. "His ruff leaks."

S

Safe: To put money in a bank account. "The Japanese safe more than we do."

Sale: To offer something for sale. "Are you going to sale your hawse?"

Sar: Not sweet. "A sweet goes goot with a sar."

Satellite: A term coined by the Pennsylwania Dutch. "Chake and Amos were awt in the fields one night when the unusual brightness of the newly launched Sputnik flew overhead. Chake said, 'Hey, Amos, satellite?' "

Sawnd: Vibrations in the air. "You hear that sawnd? Sawnds like a bird."

Scar: Scrub with cleanser. "Richard! Go scar the tub!"

Schmutz: To gunk up. "Schmutz up that axle with grease and it'll run better."

Shar: Precipitation. "April shars bring May flars."

Shooker: Sucrose. "Don't use too much shooker in that cake yet."

Shooker Scoop: The bonnet that plain women wear. "Esther looks goot in her new shooker scoop."

Shtamp: Something put on an envelope so the Post Office will mail it. "Give me a shtamp for this letter, please."

Shuffle: A tool, or the act of using that tool. "I like to shuffle the walks whenever it snows."

Shushly: Always bissy; fidgeting. "She's too shushly to chust sit and talk."

Sick and sin: Rough times. "She saw her diet through sick and sin."

Sick sack: Weave back and forth. "A skier knows haw to sick sack."

Sink: Cogitate. "Use your head to sink a little."
Also to make music with your woice: "Our choir

Sinking classical music.

prefers to sink classical music."

Site: Location. "Iss it on the right site or the left site of the road?"

Sitiate: To place; arrange. "We chust got here and we're not sitiated yet."

Slippy: A surface on which something can slide. "Walk carefully, it's slippy as a banana peel."

Smooch: Kiss. "Smooch me on the lips, you little darling."

Snack: Catch. "Did you see him snack that fly ball?"

Somesing: A particular thing. "It makes somesing dawn like a drissle."

Sop: To cry. "She softly sopped herself to sleep."

Souse: The opposite of norse. "Pam lives on the souse side of town."

Speck: Fat. "Meat with too much speck in it is heart to chew."

Spritz: Sprinkle with water. "Our Pop used to spritz us with the hose when it got too hot in the summer."

Statue: Asked of someone to determine their identity. "Hey Pete, statue?"

Still: Do it yet. "She didn't still."

Strife: Struggle. "You must strife to succeed."

Strubly: Disheveled, unkempt. "Run a comb through your strubly hair wunst."

Superwise: To direct. "Who will superwise the prochect?"

Surf: To perform an obligation. "Did you surf a big meal to your kumpny?"

T

Taar: A round piece of rubber. "The car's taars are worn out."

Tack: The art of gentle persuasion. "If you want to motivate people, you have to use a great deal of tack."

Tame people: Good people. "If tame people would leaf government to the rowdies, how would it be?"

Tar: A high structure. "When I think of Paris, I think of the Eiffel Tar."

Tawn: A small city. "I'm going to the farmer's market in tawn."

Tawsin: Ten hunerts. "It's a tawsin to one against."

Tee wee: What everybody watches. "What shows are on Tee Wee tonight?"

Telewishin: Tee Wee. "Telewishin can be an etchicational tool."

Themselfs: Those very people. "Do you think they can handle it themselfs?"

Think: An object. "What is that? I never saw a think like that before."

Thirsty: The day before Fridy. "My birthday's Thirsty."

Thistle: It'll. "Thistle do the trick."

Throttle: Spank. "Your Dad's gonna throttle you when he gets home!"

Tile: An absorbent cloth. "Rub this tile on your face and get the dirt off."

To bank: To go where the money's kept. "Why, I chust went to bank."

Togedder: Both at once. "They're going togedder."

Toiss: Playthings. "Mom! Sara's playing with my toiss again!"

Tomar: The day after today. "Tomar is another day."

Tooah: Also. "Chennie's coming tooah."

Toose: An exposed bone in the mouth used for chewing. "Isaiah lost his toose in a fight."

Toosedy: The day after Mondy. "If this is Toosedy, it must be Belgium."

Track: A parcel of land. "Are you going to build on that track of land?"

Trafel: Roam; explore. "You ken trafel through time in a good book."

Tricker: Part of a gun. "For best results don't pull the tricker; squeeze the tricker."

Trupple: Problems; no good. "His son's always in trupple."

Tuck: Pull. "Tuck the rope when you reach the bottom of the heel."

Tuck boat: A type of boat. "The tuck boats pushed the Queen Mary into the open sea."

Tum: A man's name. "Tum Sawyer is a classic."

Tum-tum: An Indian drum. "The Sioux dance to the beat of a tum-tum."

Tup: Where you bathe. "Lettie slipped in the tup and broke her hip."

Turiss: A trafler. "Did you buy this book as a turiss, or not?"

U

Udder: Something else. "I always try to look at the udder side of things."

Ukly: Terrible looking; horrible. "War is ukly."

Um: Those people or things. "Don't look at me; I don't have um."

Unner: Integrity. "On my unner, I will do my best."

Also a judge: "But Your Unner, I didn't mean to do it, unnest!"

Up: Where things get done; a general word used to help make the meaning of a sentence clear. "Clean up your plate."

"Go up to the counter and order up."

"Eat up! There's plenty more coming up!"

V

Ve: More than one of us. "Are ve going to the show?"

Vase: A piece; a little bit. "It's chust up the road a vase."

Vault: A man's name. "You ken always take your kits to see a Vault Disney moofie."

Vawtch: Look at. "Vawtch the stars at night and catch a glimpse of heffen."

Vear: To clothe. "I don't know what I'll vear on her."

Veddink: A matrimonial ceremony. "Did you get a gift for their veddink yet?"

Veed: A pest plant. "Dandelion is a veed, but we eat it yet."

Vell: A place where water is drawn. "Throw a coin in the vishing vell."

Ven: A question. "Ven is leap year next?"

Vent: Gone. "I don't know vhere the time vent!"

Verk: Labor; function. "Tum verks in a store."

Verlt var von: A big conflict. "Verlt Var Von started Verlt Var Two."

Verse: Not as good as; deteriorating. "Naomi's colt is getting verse."

Vet: Not dry. "That vet awtside will give you a cold if you don't bundle up."

Vice: Intelligent. "Benjamin Franklin was a vice man."

Vidda: A woman who has lost her husband through death.

Also, a well-known spider: "The black vidda is dangerous."

Vhy: Question the reason for. "Vhy must we fight? Vhy not peace wunst?"

Vile: During; a moment. "Come on, sit dawn and stay for a vile."

Vill: Concentration. "You can do anything if you have the vill."

Vin: Achieve victory. "Who will vin the lottery?"

Vine: Fermented grape chooce. "Chester drank all the vine."

Viper: Scrapers on a vindshield. "My vindshield vipers are screeching."

Vhistle: A shrill sawnd. "If you need me, chust vhistle."

Vood: Tree flesh. "He's a vould-be voodverker."

Vootz: A bunch of trees. "The vootz are full of animals."

Vulfes: Wild dogs. "The vulfes attacked the caribou."

W

Wacuum: Emptiness. "Nature abhors a wacuum." Also short for a wacuum cleaner: "When you're finished dusting, you ken wacuum."

Wack: Move back and forth. "My dog wacks its tail vhenever it sees me."

Walley: A space between mawntins. "Dawn in the walley, the walley so low . . ."

Walyue: Worth; the sum of. "To get the ratio, de-wide walyue one by walyue two."

Wanilla: A flavor. "Wanilla ice cream is great!"

Wary: Fluctuate. "Do you wary your routine?"

Wassleen: Petroleum jelly. "Smear wassleen on a beppy's bottom vhen it sore gets."

Wayne: Futile, to no awail. "Nick's attempt to climb the mawntin was in wayne."

Wechtapels: Carrots, peas, and such. "Our famly eats a wechtapel effry day."

Wee C.R.: A Tee Wee taping machine. "Our Wee C.R. is handy."

Wee I.P.: A big shot. "Wee I.P.s always drive in limousines."

Wee W: A make of car. "Doris has two Wee W's: a Buck and a Wan."

Wehicle: A car, truck, etc. "Is that your wehicle parked awtside?"

Went: An opening for circulation. "It was sucked in the air went."

Wery: A great deal. "Thank you wery much."

Wet: Short for wetern. "He's a Wietnam wet."

Also short for weternarian: "Your caw's sick; better call the wet."

Wice: Deputy. "What does the wice-president do, exactly?"

Wideo: Tee Wee moofies on tapes. "Do you make home wideos?"

Wifes: Maritch partners. "A bigamist has two wifes."

Wilentz: Extreme aggression. "Wilentz begets wilentz."

Willitch: A small tawn. "In the willitch by the stream lived a maiden fair."

"Go ahead, eat yourself full. You can jock it off tomar!"

Wim And Wicker: Energy. "She was so full of wim and wicker in her youth."

Wine: A long plant. "Grapes grow on wines, you dummy."

Wisit: Socialize. "Stay and wisit wunst."

With: Along. "Are you coming with?"

Also a general purpose word used to end a sentence. "This newspaper is wery good to line a cupboard with."

Wolwo: A Swedish car. "My Wolwo never lets me dawn."

Wootzer: A little pig. "Vhy you little wootzer!"

Wonders: Amazes; perplexes. "Life wonders me so."

Woted: Cast a ballot. "Haw many people woted in the last election?"

Wow: Swear; promise. "Alden and Martha exchanged wedding wows last Saturday night."

Wrench: To run water over to get the soap off. "Wrench the dishes after you wash them."

Wunst: One time. "Spread me wunst over with butter a piece of bread."

Also at a certain time. "Wunst upon a time, on a dark and stormy night . . ."

Wurst: The opposite of best. "That's the wurst show I've ever seen."

Also chopped liver. "That wurst is the best I've eaten."

X

X: Plural of eck. "Do you eat X for breakfast?"

Y

Yet: Used to end a sentence in a general way. "Is supper ready yet?" "Chakie went to the store yet." "Is it raining yet?"

Yous: Used to distinguish the plural of you. "Are yous coming with, or are chust you coming with?"

Yunk: Not olt. "The yunk ones today sure are different."

Z

Zent: A penny. "Who asked for your two zents?"

Zinc: What you wash dishes in. "Put the dishes in the zinc."

Zoop: A hot, liquid meal. "Is it zoop yet?"

For Reading Awt Lawd

In the following passages, the influence of Dutchified English is profound. They are designed to be read out loud. Some of the texts are familiar ones, so if a meaning isn't clear, look up the Standard English version. Most of the words used are not listed in the Dictionary part of this book, but by now you likely are ready for a journey into uncharted terrain, ready to make new discoveries.

Ape Lincoln's Geddysburk Address

Fourscore ent sefen yearse ago our fodders brawght forth on dis cuntinent a new nation, cunseeft in liperty, and deddicated to de proposition dat all men are crated equal.

Naw ve are engaitched in a crate ciffil var, testing vedder dat nation or enny nation so cunseeft and so deddicated ken lonk endure. Ve are met on a crate baddle feelt uff dat var. Ve haff kum to deddicate a portion uff dat feelt, aas a final rest in place fer dose who here gafe dare lifes dat dat nation might liff. It iss altogedder fittin and proper dat ve shoult do dis.

But, in a larcher sense, ve ken not deddicate, ve ken not cunsecrate, ve ken not hollow dis grawnd. Dese brafe men, liffing ent debt, who strukkled here, haff cunsecrated it, far abofe are poor par to at or detrack. Da verlt vill liddle note, nor lonk re-

Ape Lincoln

memper vhat ve say here, but it ken nefer fergit vhat day dit here. It iss fer us, da liffing, radder, to be deddicated to de unfinshed verk vhich day who fought here haff dus far so noply adwanced. It is radder fer us to be here deddicated to de crate task remainin bafore us—dat frum dese unnert debt ve take increased dewotion to dat causs for vhich dey gafe de lass full messher uff dewotion—dat ve here highly resolfe dat dese debt shall not haff dite in wayne—dat dis nation, unner Got, shall haff a new birth uff freedim—ent dat guffernmint uff da peeple, by da peeple, fer da peeple, shall not perish frum da earse.

Pletch Uff Allechintz to de Flack

I pletch allechintz to de flack uff de Unided States uff America ent to de repuplic fer vhich it stance, von nation unner Got, indiwisiple, viss liperty ent chustice fer all.

A Slection Frum Chulus Ceaser, Act Schree, Scene Twoah
Antnee's Speech to da Roamints

Frents, Roamints, Cuntrymen, Lent me your earce,
I kum to burry Ceaser, not to prase him,
De efil dat men do liffs afder dem;
De goot iss oft interrd viss dare bontz.
So led it be viss Ceaser. De nople Brudis
Hass tolt ya Ceaser vass ambitious;
Iff it ver so, it vass a griefiss fault.
Ent griefissly hass Ceaser answerdt it.
Here, unner leaf uff Brudus ent da rest,
Fer Brudis iss a hunraple man;
So dey all, all hunraple men,
Kum I ta speak inn Ceaser's funral.

First Curinsins, Chatter Sirteen, Werse Von to Sirteen.

Doe I speak wiss da tunks uff anchals, ent haff not luff, I am bekum aas sawndin brass, or a tinklin simple.

2. Ent doe I haff da giff uff proffcy, ent unnerstant all mistries, ent all knowletch, ent doe I haff face, so dat I couldt remoofe mawntins, ent haff not luff, I am nodding.

3. Ent doe I bestow all my goots to feed da pore, ent doe I giff my buddy to be burnt, ent haff not luff, it profiss me nodding.

4. Luff sufferse lonk, ent iss kindt; luff enwies not; luff vants not itselve, iss not puffed up.

5. Dust not behafe itselve unseemly, seeks not her own, iss not easely prawoked, sinks no efil.

6. Rechoyce not in niquity, but rechoyce in da truce.

7. Baress all tinks, beleafs all tinks, hopes all tinks, enduress all tinks.

8. Luff nefer failse: bud wedder dare be proffcies, dey shall fail, wedder dare be tunks, dey shall cease; wedder dare be knowletch, it shall wanish avay.

9. Fer ve knowse in part, en ve proffcy in part.

10. But ven dat vhich iss purrfict iss kum, den

dat vhich iss inn part shall be dun avay.

11. Ven I vass a childt, I spaked aas a childt, I unnerstoot aas a childt, I taught aas a childt: but ven I became a mann, I pud avay childtish sings.

12. Fer naw ve see thru a glass darkly; but den face to face, naw I noah in part, but den I shall noah efen aas also I am noan.

13. Ent naw abites face, hope, luff, dese shree, but da cratist of dese iss luff.

Haw to Haff A Goot Rummitch Sell at Your Hawse

Von: Gadder up all your olt chunk.
Twoah: Place an at in da noose paper.
Schree: Put sighnts in your yart.
Four: Vait fer buyerse to kum, ent sale dem at a goot price.
Fife: Iff it makes dawn, moofe effrysing into your crotch.

On Walyuse

You know vhat walyuse are, at least I hope you haff sum.

Mathmythins sink dat a walyue iss derifed frum dewiding walyue von into walyue two ta get walyue schree.

Dat chust ain't an at up to me, doe. My walyuse are rutted in famly, home ent church. Ent ya chust can't dewide dem. It's a whole vay uff liffin.

Naw, let's consiter ecnomic walyuse. Dutchmen are known ta be tight viss a buck, but da truce iss dat day chust know da walyue uff a buck. Vasteful peeple call frookkle peeple tight, cuss dare chelliss. Dutchmen pay cash, ent so oafer da lonk run, day haff more cuss day don't pay inntrest. Besites, ta borraw only ats ta yer sorraw.

Chust look at da farm crisiss wunst. Dutchmen don't haff enny farm crisiss. Vhy? Walyuse. Day recycle. Day uus olt tinks ven dell do, ent day don't expensife fertlizers use enny, dey chust recycle da same olt manure. Day don't pollute ent day built up radder den destroy da earse yet.

Ent de Amish don't efen hafta buy fer a rainy day insurinse, cuss iff somebuddies inn trupple, like say da barn burnt dawn, day all togedder get ent raise anudder.

Ent dat's da bickest sing in walyuse—dat ve all chust reach awt ent touch each udder viss luff. Ve'd be so happy iff ve'd chust reach awt ent touch each udder, ain't?

A Dutchified Choke

Ven in kintergarten I first learnt de alphybet, I didn't get it quite right at first. I set:

ABCDEFGIKLMNOQSTUWYZ

Da teacher looked at me funny en set, "Vhy Chunny, vere's da H?"
I set, "Vhy teacher, you noah my H. It's fife."
"Den vere's da chay?"
"Aut dare, on da tree."
"Den vere's da P?"
"It's running dawn my leck."
"Ent vere's da R?"
"Up dare. On da vall. It's schree o'clock."
"Ent vere's da V?"
"Vhy teacher, V all here!"
"Ent vere's da X?"
"I hat dem fer breakfist. Dare all."

A Liddle Sumsing Extra

Haw naw brawn caw?

A Day in the Life of Johnny Huckenduppler

My name is Johnny Huckenduppler and I thought I'd try to write without an accent a day in the life of a Dutchman. I get it out a little funny sometimes, but I hope you understand.

It wonders me so how life goes. Today I was out in the field throwing the horse over the fence some hay after I had loaded the wagon off and shut the gate wide open. Amos Oberholtzer called me to the fence over to talk down a ways. We live neighbors to the Oberholtzers and our fields meet yet. They live on the hill a little up, out where the road gives a fork and then gets all.

Amos told me how he and Sarah went to Lancaster the other day and walked the town all over just to schnoz around. Amos bought some new shoes there, but he said they walked heavy so he took them back. Now it makes a body weary to hear of such dull going ons, so I told Amos I didn't have my chores caught after and I haven't the time to dopple. Amos said he could see I was already busy yet, so he told me to come down and visit them a little once some day soon. I said, "Sure, when we come the road up, we'll come over." He said, "Great, come ahead back once."

The horse was thirsty yet so I pumped myself from the well a bucket of water. My son Jacob came to sit the horse on. After he a little rode, he said, "I want down here off." Then he ran back to the house to take dinner, but on the way he ouched. I ran over to see the matter. Here he had stung his foot with a bee.

I picked him up and quick ran to the front house door. I couldn't make the door open because the lock was on. Then yet the button didn't bell, so I bumped hard the door. My wife Katie was with a vacuum sweeping the floor down, and didn't hear us. So I quick went the hind way round and got into the kitchen there. I smeared Jacob's foot all over with salve and he simmered down.

Katie ran in all ferhoodled. She looked at Jacob and said, "Ach, you look bad in the foot. You look wonderful sick. Don't you feel so good? Does it ouch you so in the foot?" She asked so many questions so fast I had to say, "Don't talk so quick—it runs together when I think."

The swelling went down as we sat ourselves awhile. Katie kissed Jacob and he said, "Mom, you're wonderful nice." She start smooching me then too, but I was hungry instead, so I said, "Kissing wears out, cooking don't."

"Well, why don't you eat yourself out more often then?" she said.

"I make the hay, you make the meals," I said. "I would rather single live than the wife the britches give."

"You ought yourself to shame," Katie said quick. "Cows come and cows go, but the bull in this house keeps coming."

She was right. I didn't want to grow too soon old and too late smart. I knew I'd better put myself other ways on. Katie learned me this, over and over.

Katie wears herself plain. But it makes me no difference. She's a good wife—she knows me yet she loves me.

We nixed our argument with a good smooch and hugged all over. I was manury from the fields yet, so upstairs I hurried and spritzed myself all over in the shower and clean became. Then I combed myself once because I was all strubbly. Katie finished redding up the house and started supper yet.

Jacob came out of his room when I was finished with myself combing. Down the stairs together we came with.

"What does it give for supper?" asked Jacob.

"I'm bad for pot pie," I said.

In the kitchen the Lebanon Bologna pot pie with heat was on the table boiling. Katie knew my hungries.

"Throw your Pop down from the cupboard some glasses," Katie said to Jacob.

I then poured us from the jug of birch beer three glasses.

Jacob drank some and said while he was still drinking, so it came out all bubbly, "This glass sure drinks wonderful good."·

"Before you speak, drink your mouth empty," said Katie. "Now seat yourself down and set yourself for good eating. Supper's fixed."

I dug in too quick with hunger. The pot pie was hot and my tongue I burned. On my shirt I dropped some.

"Tuck yourself under the chin this napkin," said Katie.

I blowed the pot pie cool on my plate and wootzed it down.

"Don't eat yourself full, Pop, there's shoo-fly pie back," said Jacob.

"Well this pot pie eats so good, I must eat it all."

After we had done and Jacob went to bed, Katie looked at me and winked. "Well, the food is all but the best is yet."

We outened the lights and went up the wooden hill to the bedroom. It was making down outside and probably would continue tomorrow down.

But who cares about the rain? I thought as I climbed in the bed with Katie.

It looks for a pretty good night tonight.

To Be Sunk Awt Lawd
(For your sinking enchoyment)

O Liddle Tawn of Besselhem

O Liddle tawn of Besselhem,
Haw still ve see dee lie,
Abofe die deep ent dreamless sleep,
De silent starse go by.
Yet in de dark streets shiness
An efferlasting light,
Da hopes ent fearse uff all da yearse,
Are met in zee tonight.

Chinkle Belse

Vile dashing thru da snow
Inn a von horse open sleigh,
Oafer da feelts vill go
Laffink all da vay.
Da belse on boptail rink
Day make our spirits bright,
Vhat fun it iss to write ent sink
A sleighing sonk tonight.

Chinkle belse, chinkle belse,
Chinkle all da vay,
Oh! vhat fun it iss to write
Inn a von horse open sleigh.

Dawn in de Walley

Dawn in de walley, de walley so low,
Hank yer het oafer, hear de vint blow,
Hear de vint blow, dear, hear de vint blow,
Hank yer het oafer, hear de vint blow.

Writing dis ledder, containing schree lines,
Answer my quvestion, vill you be mine?
Vill you be mine, dear, vill you be mine?
Answer my quvestion, vill you be mine?

Roases luff sunshine, wiolets luff dew,
Anchels in heffen, know I luff you.
Know I luff you, dear, know I luff you,
Anchels in heffen, know I luff you.

Receipts
(Dese receipts really make)

Cussin Rachel's Snitz und Knepp

Ven you eat this finished, drawn in varm milk ent sprinkle on nutmeck. But cook yourself as follaws first.

Cook von pawnd bakin from a pick fer schree ares. Chently simmer von qwart sveet drite apfels viss da peel leafed on in vater smuddered. Ven da bakin iss cooked, in togedder day go for anudder are. Vile dis iss on da stofe cookin, make da net like so: Mix togedder schree cups flar, two bick teasespoonse uff bakin pawder, a liddle salt to taste, break in two X, mix in milk enuff to make the badder stiff. On de apfels drop spoonfulse uff de batter until cuffert. Put back on da lit and for a few minutes cook yet; den drop effry naw ent den sum more badder till you're used up.

Keep boiling viss enuff vater to prewent yourselve frum burnin.

Rhett Beet X

Boil a dussen beets until dare tendericed, but not mushy yet, den plunch dem into colt vater so off kum da skints.

Boil da following mix up: Von-halve cup vater, Von-halve teasespoonse salt, Von-halve ent von cup winegar, two cups shooker.

Boil dis mix up in da stofe immersed, until da beets get varm but not yet bolt. At some raw unt-yents and dill for spice. Don't cofer da chars yet after you pourt da mix up in, cuss ve haff to put in da X yet.

Shell da whole, heart-bolt X into da rhett beet mix-up abofe. Iff you like a fancy touch, put yourself in a cinnamin stick. Naw cofer da char ent use after picklin' for two dayse.

A Goot Cha-Cha

At de market get fresh qwart uff green pepperse, ent von qwart rhett pepperse, schree qwarts green ent rhett tomaters mixed up, schree qwarts green cucumpers, schree qwarts small unyents, halve peck uff strink beance, four or fife carits cuped, von larch cabbitch het ent cauliflar, a punch uff liddle rawnd peace for pretty (awt uff da peace pot uff course), a corn on da cop (viss da corn knifed off da cop uff course), sum lima beance to fill awt, ent sum udder such sings for your own creation to make. Slice up all no more than liddle pieces abawt a sird uff a inch sick, ent boil da wechtaples indi-witchally ent set the night oafer. In de morning strain dem. Place effrysing in chars all mixed up.

Make da herp choose, as follaws: Von pawnd musturt seat, von-halve pawnd allspice, von-halve pawnd black pepper, teasespoon uff vite clofe, two uff celry seats, von pawnd brawn shooker (leaf awt iff ya vant it sar), sum liddle tumric, sum curry pawder. Viss von gallon uff winegar ent von pint chighan brine mix. For sirty minutes boil heart ent den oafer da wechtaples pour. At winegar to desi-redt sickness.

Let it stant oafer night. Enchoy da next day.

Chighan Pot Pie

Cut a yunk chighan up into pieces ent into boilt vater put dem ent cook until tender. Keep it vell drawned. Vile da chighan boilse neat togedder da nootles ingredience: 2 X vell beat up, 2 busser ta-plespoonse, 2 cups flar, some milk ent salt. Blent togedder da flar ent busser, at salt ent da X ent chust enuff milk to make the dough a liddle stiff. Bafore leading it stant for an are, roll it awt as sin as it won't tear. Cut it into some sqvares as bic as you like yourself viss somesing sharp. Meanvile scrup all dese wechtaples den do dis to dem:

Peel schree potaters den slice dem into cupes. At abawt a dussen carits or so ent at sum parsely for pretty. If da peace are still in da pot, remoofe dem awt, else chust put da peace in. At sum unyents to taste.

Ven da chighan iss tendericed for sure, den layer all dese goot sinks in a larch kettle dat's bic enuff. At salt ent pepper ent saffron ent tumeric a liddle. Cuffer tight after da boiling chighan bross iss pourt oafer all. Simmer fer an are.

Serf it haw ya likes.

Notaple Wariations: Supstitute Sawsitch or Lepnin Boloney or beef for da chighan abofe. Eats goot tooah!

Bret Filling

Von loaf vite bret or rye or whole veat
Sefen taplespoonse uff busser or marchrin
Von-half cup unyent
Fife X beaten up
Four qwarts milk
Von teasespoon salt
Sum pepper ent saffrin

Crack X into meshrin cup vile de unyents in

sum marchrin slowly cook. At sum milk ent beat altogedder viss da bret ent da ceasenins. Pour inta a larch creased bacon dish.

Bake abawt an are or so at 300 decrees.

Enchoy yourself viss dis dishent sum udder sinks, like turkey, tooah.

Grossmommy Esther's Anchel Saladt

8 apfels
2 nanas
½ cup chopped celry
½ cup raisints
1 crated rindt uff lemin

1 taplespoon cornstarch
⅔ cup pineapfel choose
1 eck
2 taplespoonse shooker
1 bunch uff purple crepes

Chop da marshmellers vich veren't menchint abofe, nanas ent crepes ent pineapfel. Mix da marshmellers ent fruit up; den at de crushed nuts somevears. Make a cooked dressin uff de eck, shooker ent cornstarch ent pineapfel choose. Cool da dressink ent at de vipped cream. Combine viss saladt mixture ent surf on lettuce.

Surfs sefen if liddle, fife iff bick.

Qvick ent Easee Futch

1 pawnd pawdert shooker
½ cup peanit busser
½ cup coco
½ pawnd melted busser or marchrin
Pinch uff salt
Shot uff wanilla

Mix togedder vell unt put in a shallow schmutzed up pan. Cool for seffral ares.

Hamburker ent Eck Nootles

4 awntz eck nootles (Cook ent drain yourself first)
1 can cream uff chighan zoup
1 cup milk
2 cups cooked hamburker
½ cup rhett or green or bose chopped pepperse

Put cheese oafer abofe ent bake at 350 decrees for a half are. Eat ven hunkry.

Abawt the Author

Gary Gates is a Dutchman from Lebanon County, Pennsylvania. He loves speaking fun English, but often lapses into conventional speech just for the comfort of conformity.

His dream is to become a full-time writer. This book is a first step in that direction.

With a previous book, a publisher told him to rewrite it in standard English, without the Dutchisms. "Unless, of course," laughed the publisher, "everyone starts speaking Dutchified English."

This book seizes the challenge.

The author is currently working on an **Adwanced Wersion, Wolume Two**, of **How to Speak Dutchified English**. He would appreciate contributions to this project. Please send your favorite Dutchified words, phrases, jokes, stories, receipts, or anything else you feel would be of value to:

Gary Gates c/o Good Books
Main Street, Intercourse, PA 17534

Because of expected volume of replies, no personal acknowledgment or payment of any kind will be possible. Thank you!